# LIVING IN THE WILD: BIG CATS

# CHEETAHS

**Charlotte Guillain**

raintree

a Capstone company — publishers for children

Raintree is an imprint of Capstone Global Library Limited, a company incorporated in England and Wales having its registered office at 7 Pilgrim Street, London, EC4V 6LB – Registered company number: 6695582

www.raintreepublishers.co.uk
myorders@raintreepublishers.co.uk

Edited by Clare Lewis and Adrian Vigliano
Designed by Tim Bond
Original illustrations © HL Studios
Picture research by Tracy Cummins
Originated by Capstone Global Library Ltd
Printed and bound in China

ISBN 978 1 406 27342 7 (hardback)
17 16 15 14 13
10 9 8 7 6 5 4 3 2 1

ISBN 978 1 406 27349 6 (paperback)
18 17 16 15
10 9 8 7 6 5 4 3 2 1

A full catalogue record for this book is available from the British Library.

**Acknowledgements**
We would like to thank the following for permission to reproduce photographs: Getty Images pp. 5 (Heinrich van den Berg), 18 (Manoj Shah), 23 (Ben Cranke), 34 (James Warwick), 35 (Visuals Unlimited, Inc./Joe McDonald), 37 (Steven L. Raymer/National Geographic), 39 (John Warburton-Lee), 43 (Gerry Ellis), 45 (Mike Hill); Shutterstock pp. 6 (Stu Porter), 7 (Yuri Gupta), 9 (Sue Green), 11 (Jason Prince), 13 (Johan Barnard), 15 (David W Hughes), 16 (Jerome Scholler), 17 (JI de Wet), 19 (Karel Gallas), 20 (Mogens Trolle), 25 (Simon Clay), 27 (Gary Unwin), 28 (zahorec), 29 (Stu Porter), 31 (HPH Image Library), 33 (Oleg Znamenskiy); Superstock pp. 12 (Minden Pictures), 22 (Thomas Dressler / age footstock), 24 (Suzi Eszterhas/Minden Pictures), 41 (NHPA), 42 (Minden Pictures).

Cover photograph of a cheetah reproduced with permission of Superstock (Gerard Lacz/age footstock).

We would like to thank Michael Bright for his invaluable help in the preparation of this book.

Every effort has been made to contact copyright holders of any material reproduced in this book. Any omissions will be rectified in subsequent printings if notice is given to the publisher.

**Disclaimer**

# Contents

Some words are shown in bold, **like this**. You can find out what they mean by looking in the glossary.

# What are big cats?

In the long, dry grass of the African **savannah**, a stealthy shape creeps towards a herd of antelope. A moment later, a cheetah bursts into action, chasing a small antelope at top speed. The cheetah's **prey** cannot outrun it and the slender cat brings it down. The cat will not go hungry today.

Cheetahs are mammals that are often included in a group called big cats. The general term 'big cat' refers to wild cats that are significantly larger than small wild cats, such as the lynx, serval, and ocelot. These larger cats include cheetahs, pumas, jaguars, lions, tigers, leopards, snow leopards, and clouded leopards. However, sometimes the term big cat is used more specifically to refer to large wild cats that can roar: lions, tigers, leopards, and jaguars. Cheetahs are unable to roar and both look and behave quite differently from other big cats.

The wider group of big cats shares the following characteristics:

- They are all above a certain size.
- They are all carnivores.
- None of them is hunted for food by another **predator** once they reach adulthood.

Big cats live in different habitats around the world, ranging from the rainforests of South America to African grasslands and the mountains of Southeast Asia. Some, such as leopards, can climb trees while others, such as tigers, are strong swimmers. Lions are the only big cats to routinely live in groups, called prides. All big cats have colouring or patterns on their fur that help to conceal them as they hunt.

## SPOTTY CAT

The word 'cheetah' comes from the Hindu word *chita*, meaning 'spotted one'.

The cheetah looks quite different from other big cats, with its long, slim build and small head.

5

# What are cheetahs?

The cheetah has a long, slim body and long tail, often with a white tuft of hair on the tip. Its yellowish-brown fur is covered in a black spotted pattern, with whiter fur on its belly. A cheetah's eyes are a golden yellow with distinctive black markings running from the inside of each eye to the edge of the mouth.

Male cheetahs tend to be slightly bigger than females, standing around 75 centimetres (29.5 inches) tall. Their length of around 1.2 metres (4 feet) and weight of up to 54 kilograms (119 pounds) make them one of the smaller big cats. Cheetahs are well known for their speed, which can reach 114 kilometres (71 miles) per hour in about three seconds! They are faster than any other land animal.

A cheetah's powerful legs help it reach amazing speeds in only a few seconds.

## ALMOST EXTINCT

Some scientists think that cheetahs almost became extinct around 10,000 years ago, during the Ice Age. The animals survived but there were very few animals left to **reproduce**. This means their descendants – today's cheetahs – are all closely related. Because of this, the whole cheetah population is at risk from the same diseases or changes to their habitat.

# Cheetah evolution

Around 20,000 years ago, several **species** of cheetah lived around the world. Scientists think they evolved in Africa and later migrated to Asia and beyond. By around 10,000 years ago, only one species of cheetah remained. Gradually cheetahs gained adaptations, which helped them survive where they lived. An **adaptation** is a feature that allows an animal to live in a particular way in a particular place. Adaptations arise as species **evolve** over thousands of years. (See pages 12 to 17 for more information on cheetah adaptations.)

The distinctive cheetah 'tear' eye markings can be seen here.

# How are cheetahs classified?

All living things are put into groups, or **classified**, by scientists. This helps to identify every living thing accurately and to explain how and why they live where they do. Classification means grouping living things according to the features that they share.

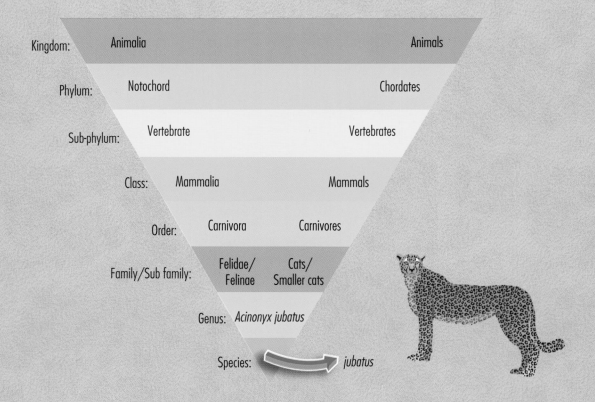

| | | |
|---|---|---|
| Kingdom: | Animalia | Animals |
| Phylum: | Notochord | Chordates |
| Sub-phylum: | Vertebrate | Vertebrates |
| Class: | Mammalia | Mammals |
| Order: | Carnivora | Carnivores |
| Family/Sub family: | Felidae/Felinae | Cats/Smaller cats |
| Genus: | *Acinonyx jubatus* | |
| Species: | *jubatus* | |

This pyramid shows how the cheetah is classified. The scientific name *Acinonyx* means 'unmovable claw', while *jubatus* means 'maned' or 'crested'. Cheetah cubs have a distinctive crest of hair.

The leopard is in the same family (Felidae) as the cheetah. Leopards are much bigger and more powerful than cheetahs.

## Classification groups

Classification triangles are used to show how each living thing is classified. Towards the bottom of the triangle, each group contains fewer and fewer members. For example, there are fewer animals in the order Carnivora (carnivores) than there are in the class Mammalia (mammals), and so on.

Cheetahs are in the family Felidae, which includes all cats, large and small, wild and domesticated.

Living things are given a Latin name, such as *Acinonyx jubatus*, so they have a single name rather than many different names in different languages. The cheetah is also a member of the sub-family Felinae, and so is related to all the smaller cats, such as the lynx, serval, and the domestic pet cat.

Cheetahs are unique among the cats because they have their own genus, *Acinonyx*. They are the only species in this genus. Sometimes living things are grouped into subspecies within a species because of small differences between them, but there is only one species of cheetah.

# Where do cheetahs live?

All wild animals live in a **habitat**. This is the place where an animal can find everything it needs to live, such as food, water, and shelter. A cheetah's typical habitat is grasslands and open plains, but they can also be found in rocky uplands and woodlands. Today, most cheetahs live in Namibia and Botswana, with other large populations in East Africa.

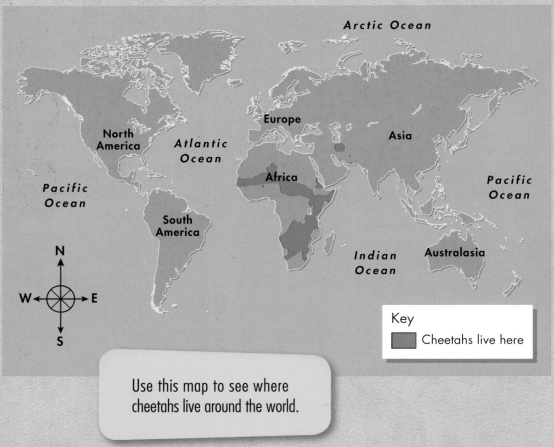

Arctic Ocean

Europe

North America

Asia

Atlantic Ocean

Africa

Pacific Ocean

Pacific Ocean

South America

Indian Ocean

Australasia

N
W E
S

Key
Cheetahs live here

Use this map to see where cheetahs live around the world.

## ASIAN CHEETAHS

Cheetahs used to live across the Middle East and Asia but the loss of suitable habitats and prey led to a huge drop in their numbers. Today the only known cheetahs living in the wild outside Africa are in Iran. Scientists think there are as few as 70 to 110 cheetahs left there. The Iranian government is now working with various international organizations to help protect these animals. There have also been unconfirmed sightings of cheetahs in an area of Pakistan near the Iranian border.

## Finding food

The large African grasslands, for example on the Serengeti Plain in Tanzania, East Africa, have provided a perfect habitat for cheetahs for thousands of years. Grass-eating animals, such as antelope, live on the plains in large herds. They **migrate**, or travel, following the rains and new grass. Cheetahs hunt these prey animals for food and so need to live in a habitat that supports them. Each adult cheetah must have an area of land between 800 and 1,500 square kilometres (310 and 581 square miles) to find all the food and water it needs. Long grasses also offer a good hiding place for a mother cheetah's cubs, to protect them as she hunts.

# What adaptations help cheetahs survive?

A cheetah has many adaptations to help it catch prey. Its incredible speed allows it to chase down fast-moving prey. The cheetah's slender frame makes it light, while its flexible **spine**, hips, and shoulders allow it to twist and change direction as it chases prey. Its long tail helps with balance as it turns in different directions at high speed.

## Long legs

The cheetah's long legs are perfectly adapted to take very long strides, as is its long, flexible spine. When it runs, the cheetah only ever has one foot on the ground at a time, its legs swinging in and then extending out as it speeds forward.

It's possible for a running cheetah to travel 7 to 8 metres (23 to 26 feet) in just one stride!

A cheetah can chase even the fastest prey as it darts and dodges away.

## Paws and claws

Just as a sprinting athlete wears special spiked shoes, a cheetah's feet are perfectly suited to running fast. While other cats have to pull out their claws when they need to use them, the cheetah's claws always stick out. Their job is not to hold onto prey, like a tiger's long, sharp claws. A cheetah's short, blunt claws grip the ground as it runs, helping it to move faster. Its hard paw pads also help grip by acting in a similar way to treads on a car tyre.

### VAN PHILLIPS

Van Phillips is an American engineer who came up with the idea of designing running blades for **amputee** athletes. He based his design on the curved shape of a cheetah's back legs. The first blades that were manufactured were called 'Cheetahs'.

## Built for speed

To run at such fast speeds, a cheetah needs plenty of **oxygen** moving around its body. It has adaptations, such as large nostrils and **sinuses**, to breathe in large amounts of air. The oxygen in the air moves into the cheetah's extra big lungs before being carried around its body in large arteries to reach the cheetah's muscles quickly. The blood carrying this oxygen is pumped around the body by a large and powerful heart. The cheetah also has an extra-large liver, which can store energy for when it is needed. These adaptations allow the cheetah to run in incredibly intense bursts of speed, but it can't run far before it becomes tired. Most chases only last around 20 seconds.

## Keeping cool

Cheetahs hunt during the day when the sun is still up. They also use a large amount of energy running at such high speeds and so it's important that they don't get too hot. They have several adaptations to help them keep cool. A cheetah's slim body and thin fur help to prevent it overheating as it hunts. After a fast burst of running, cheetahs pant like dogs and sweat through their paws to lose heat. In addition to these adaptations, cheetahs will also often rest in the shade for a long time after a chase to cool down.

### SUPER SENSES

A cheetah's senses are adapted to hunt prey. Its powerful eyes can see up to 5 kilometres (3 miles) away. Cheetahs also have excellent hearing and a strong sense of smell to help locate prey.

The black marks around a cheetah's eyes may help to protect its eyes from the glare of bright sunlight.

15

## Out of sight

Because a cheetah isn't able to run after prey for a long distance, like all cats it uses the element of surprise when hunting, and creeps up on its prey unseen. The sandy colouring of its fur, with its black spotted pattern, helps to **camouflage** the cheetah as it hides in the long, dry grass and among bushes and trees close to prey. Camouflage is also important to keep cheetah cubs safe. While their mother hunts, young cubs can be hidden in the long grass to protect them from other predators. Cheetah cubs are very vulnerable when they are young and so this adaptation may be crucial in keeping them alive.

### SPOTS, STRIPES, AND RINGS

Every cheetah has a unique pattern of spots on its coat and special black rings towards the end of its tail. Some cheetahs have more blotchy patterns on their coats, where the spots have merged together into stripe-like markings. These are known as 'king cheetahs'. Scientists think the blotchy markings are caused by a **genetic** change and believe that markings on a domestic tabby cat are caused in the same way.

A cheetah's colouring helps it to hide as it creeps up on its prey.

## No competition

The cheetah is much smaller than other big predators on the grasslands, such as lions and leopards. It is adapted to hunt during the daytime, while other big cats tend to hunt at night. This means it doesn't have to compete with the other hunters and has a better chance of keeping a kill, as bigger animals who could easily steal from a cheetah tend to be asleep when it hunts.

# What do cheetahs eat?

Like other cats, the cheetah is a carnivore, only eating meat that it has hunted and killed itself. It tends to eat mammals, particularly smaller antelope, such as Thompson's gazelle, impala, and springbok. Cheetahs will also eat the young of larger antelope, as well as rabbits, birds, and warthogs.

## Hunting

The cheetah uses its eyes to find suitable prey. It sits on high points, such as termite mounds, to scan the landscape around it before selecting prey and approaching through the long grass. A cheetah will only move in for the kill when it is close enough to its prey to catch it after a short, intense run. When the cheetah has caught up with its prey, it trips its victim by hooking the back legs with a swipe of its front paw. There is a large, curved **dewclaw** on this paw, which helps to trip prey up. The cheetah then moves in for the kill by biting its prey on the neck, strangling it. The cheetah is very tired at this point but it has to keep hold of its struggling prey until it has suffocated.

This cheetah is trying to trip up a large hartebeest antelope with its front paws during a chase.

Cheetahs creep along, trying to get as close as they can to their prey before the chase.

## CHEETAH EYES

Unlike other cats, cheetahs don't have good night vision. Their eyesight is useful, however, for hunting in daylight. The cheetah has a short **muzzle** and large eyes positioned on the front of its face. This gives the cheetah strong **binocular vision**, where it uses both eyes together. It can also judge distances accurately, which helps it to get as close to prey as possible before starting to run.

Cheetahs eat as quickly as they can after making a successful kill.

## Feeding

Only around half a cheetah's chases result in a successful kill. The cheetah is exhausted after killing its victim. A single cheetah is also unable to keep a large kill to eat over several days because it can't hide or protect it from **scavengers**, such as hyenas. Because of this, a cheetah needs to eat very quickly after it has caught its breath and cooled down after a kill, before it attracts other animals.

## WATER FROM FOOD

Cheetahs only need to drink water from a waterhole or river every three to four days. They get the rest of the water they need from the prey they eat.

# Cheetah food web

All animals have to eat plants or other animals to live and they, in turn, may be eaten by other animals. This is called a **food chain**. The energy in a food chain starts with the sun. Plants use the sun's energy to make food and are called **producers**. Animals are called **consumers** because they consume (eat) plants or other animals. Animals that eat plants for energy (herbivores) make up the next link in the food chain. These include the antelope eaten by cheetahs. Carnivores, such as the cheetah, make up the next link in the food chain, getting their energy from the animals they eat. Many connected food chains make up a **food web**.

Cheetah

Rabbit

Gazelle

Grass

Leaves

This is a food web. The arrows go from the plant or animal being eaten to the animal that eats it. In this food web, gazelles and rabbits eat plants. Cheetahs eat gazelles and rabbits.

# What is a cheetah's life cycle?

An animal's life cycle is the stages it goes through from birth to death. A cheetah's life cycle goes through three main stages: birth, youth, and adulthood. Cheetahs reach adulthood when they are old enough to reproduce and have cubs themselves.

## Meeting and mating

Adult male and female cheetahs live in separate areas and only come together to **mate**. This usually happens during the dry season but can happen at any time of year if a female is ready to mate. Females are around 22 months old when this happens, while male cheetahs are ready to mate around the age of two and half years. Sometimes several males will fight over one female.
A female cheetah's pregnancy lasts for 90 to 95 days.

## Birth of cubs

Just before giving birth to cubs, a mother cheetah finds a nest in a quiet place, hidden by long grass or rocks. She gives birth to several cubs, often around five but sometimes as many as eight. The tiny cubs can weigh as little as 250 grams (about eight ounces) and their eyes are closed.

Cheetah cubs completely depend on their mother to protect and feed them.

A female cheetah keeps away from males apart from when she is ready to mate.

## BABY CHEETAHS

Newborn cubs have dark fur with their spots merged together. As they develop, they grow tufty hair on their backs, called a **mantle**. This is useful for camouflage in the dry grass. Some scientists think it also helps to protect the cubs from heavy rain and the hot sun. The cubs lose most of the mantle by the time they are three months old, but some tufts remain around their neck until they reach adulthood.

## Cub development

When the cubs are around a week old, their eyes open and they start to move around inside the nest. They depend on their mother's milk for food. Their teeth appear after three weeks. Their mother often carries the cubs in her mouth to different nesting sites so that predators won't start to smell them. The cubs stay hidden for five or six weeks, until they are big enough to follow their mother and start to eat meat. They stop drinking milk altogether around three months after birth.

## Staying safe

Life is very dangerous for cheetah cubs. In some areas, as many as 90 per cent of cubs are killed by larger predators, such as lions, wild dogs, and hyenas, before they reach the age of three months. The cubs' mother tries to protect them by hiding them in long grass as she hunts, but she can be gone for a long time and sometimes loses them. If cubs face danger when their mother is near, she will defend them fiercely, despite her small size. She will attempt to fight off leopards and hyenas but is unlikely to take on a lion.

Like all young mammals, cheetah cubs feed on their mother's milk.

Cheetah cubs will stay where their mother has hidden them until she returns.

## POPULATION THREAT

Although it seems very sad that so many cheetah cubs are killed at a young age, scientists studying cheetah populations have found that these deaths are not as much of a threat to the species' survival as deaths of adult cheetahs. When a mother cheetah loses her cubs, she tends to reproduce again very quickly. It is more important that conservationists protect adult cheetahs as they are needed to keep population numbers growing.

# How do cheetahs behave?

## Hunting lessons

Like all cats, cheetah cubs learn to hunt by watching their mother and playing with each other. At first they only observe their mother hunting but by the time they are around seven months old they start to join in. Their mother will start to let them make the final kill after she has knocked prey down and eventually they are ready to hunt on their own.

## Independence

Cheetah cubs are ready to leave their mother when they are able to hunt for their own food. This usually happens when they are around 14 to 18 months old. The young females tend to live and hunt alone except for when they are raising cubs, while male cheetahs often live with their brothers or other males in groups called **coalitions**. They can stay together in these groups for life.

### GRÉGOIRE BOUGUEREAU

Grégoire Bouguereau is a French wildlife photographer who spent almost ten years observing cheetahs in the Serengeti National Park in Tanzania. He took an award-winning photograph showing a mother cheetah giving her cubs a hunting lesson. The mother had caught a gazelle calf but didn't kill it. Instead, she left the injured calf near her cubs and waited for them to catch it as it tried to escape. Bouguereau's photograph captures the four cubs watching the gazelle intently as it tries to escape them.

| Cat | Lifespan in the wild |
| --- | --- |
| Cheetah | around 12 years |
| Lion | around 15 years |
| Jaguar | around 15 years |
| Leopard | around 15 years |
| Puma | around 20 years |
| Tiger | around 20 years |

This chart shows the lifespan of some big cats in the wild.

Cheetahs that survive into adulthood have a typical lifespan of between seven and twelve years.

A coalition of male cheetahs will establish their own **territory**, where there is plenty of prey to hunt. Male cheetahs will defend their territory from other males to ensure there is enough food to survive. They do this by scent-marking their territory with **urine** and marking their area in other ways, such as clawing at the ground or tree bark, or leaving **faeces** in prominent places. These markings warn other male cheetahs not to enter their territory. Any intruders who disregard these warnings will be attacked.

Solitary female cheetahs are not territorial but hunt across a large **home range**. This can be as large as 800 square kilometres (308 square miles) and could cover several male cheetah territories.

## CHEETAH SOUNDS

Cheetahs can't roar like the larger big cats. They do make a range of other sounds, including a chirping noise that a mother and cubs use to communicate with each other. Cheetahs also make growling, yowling, purring, snarling, and hissing noises.

This male cheetah is scent-marking his territory.

## Daytime activity

Unlike most other big cats, cheetahs are **diurnal** hunters. While lions and leopards tend to hunt and become more active at night and have excellent night vision, cheetahs are most active during the day and cannot see well in the dark. At the hottest time of year, cheetahs hunt in the early morning or evening when the temperature is cooler but there is enough light to locate and stalk prey. In the cooler season, they hunt throughout the day.

### ROAMING MALES

Some male cheetahs don't keep their own territory but constantly roam around in other cheetahs' areas. These non-territorial males are usually younger cheetahs that have recently left their mothers, or older males.

# A DAY IN THE LIFE OF A CHEETAH

Cheetahs wake up early in the morning. If the cheetah is hungry, then it is ready to hunt as soon as the sun comes up. A mother cheetah might take older cubs with her to teach them how to hunt and kill. It might take several chases to succeed in killing some prey and then the cheetah must eat quickly before scavengers, such as hyenas, smell the fresh meat. A cheetah will normally eat up to 14 kilograms (30 pounds) of meat in one sitting. Then it abandons what is left of its kill and will not need to eat again for a few days, unless it is a mother needing to feed cubs.

## Resting and playing

As the day starts to get warmer, cheetahs normally rest in the shade to avoid the sun's heat. Cubs will wrestle and play with each other as an important part of learning how to hunt. Cheetahs will sleep to save energy and **groom** themselves for hours by licking each other's faces. A cheetah's tongue is covered in rough, hook-like bumps called papillae that remove dirt from fur when it licks itself. After eating, a mother and her cubs will often spend time making sure their faces and paws are clean.

## Eating and drinking

As evening draws in, cheetahs that have not eaten recently will look for prey. They may visit a waterhole or river if they are thirsty and need to drink. Then, as night falls, cheetahs go to sleep in a safe, sheltered spot. They have a long sleep during the night.

Cheetahs need to spend a lot of time resting in the shade to conserve energy and recover from hunting.

# How intelligent are cheetahs?

It is difficult to identify and measure what we know as intelligence in animals. Much of the way they behave is based on **instinct** as much as intelligence. However, cheetahs seem to demonstrate intelligent behaviour in several ways that are crucial to their survival.

## Communication

A mother cheetah and her cubs, or males within a coalition, need to communicate well to protect each other and work as a team. Scientists observing cheetahs have identified different sounds with different meanings. For example, chirping is used to find hidden or lost cubs and by adults greeting each other. Cubs also chirp to show excitement after a kill. Cheetahs hiss or moan when their prey is taken by bigger animals and they bleat when in distress. Cheetahs that are resting or grooming together will often purr loudly to show contentment.

Cheetahs greet each other using touch, such as cheek rubbing and face licking. Cheetahs also communicate using smells. They can recognize if intruders have entered their territory by smelling urine or faeces that they don't recognize. A female cheetah that is ready to mate will scent-mark with urine to attract males.

## Staying safe

Cheetahs are among the smaller predators in their habitat and are vulnerable when larger carnivores are nearby. Cheetahs know they have a better chance of staying safe by running away or hiding when big predators threaten to take their kill. Mother cheetahs also hide cubs carefully so they won't be spotted by hyenas or lions. A mother cheetah might act as a **decoy** to draw threats away.

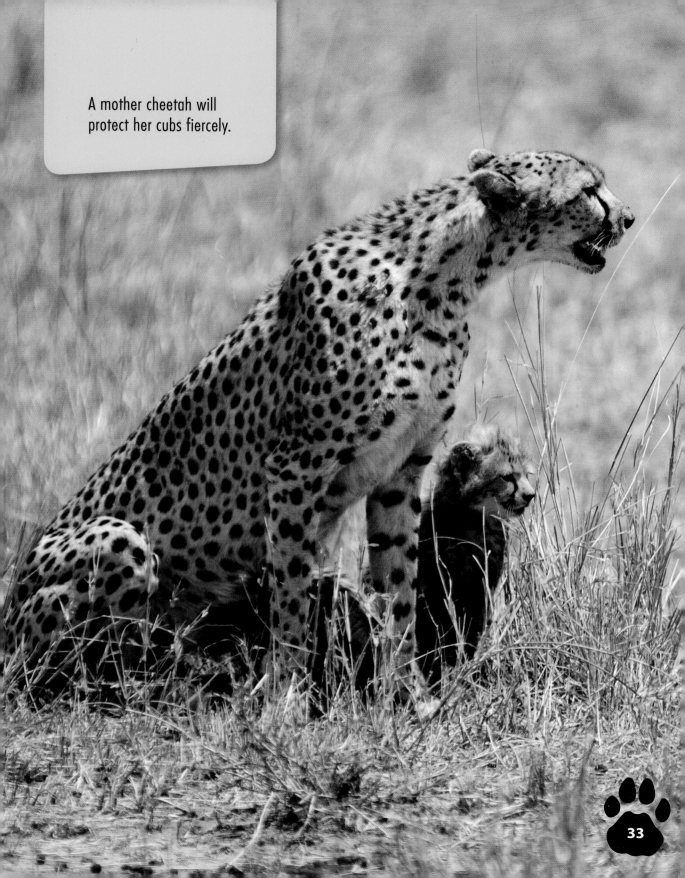

A mother cheetah will protect her cubs fiercely.

## Teamwork

Although cheetahs typically hunt and kill prey on their own, some male cheetahs in coalitions will work as a team to catch larger prey. A group of cheetahs can bring down larger prey than a single cheetah, such as a wildebeest, zebra, or even an ostrich. They have to communicate to target the same victim and attack from different angles. Then their combined strength is enough to hold down and overpower their prey, while as a group they have more chance of defending their kill from scavengers.

## Learned behaviour

Another sign of an animal's intelligence is how it is able to learn new behaviours. All cheetahs learn how to hunt and stay safe from threats when they are cubs. Mother cheetahs take great care to show their cubs useful survival skills and will gradually involve them more and more in hunting until they are ready to find and kill prey on their own.

A group of cheetahs can hunt for larger prey and share a successful kill.

This mother cheetah is teaching her cub how to stalk prey.

## SIMON KING

Simon King is a wildlife filmmaker who has spent over 20 years observing and filming big cats in the wild. He cared for a pair of cheetah cubs whose mother was killed by a lion when they were only four weeks old. Cubs learn everything they need to know to survive from their mother, so Simon had to teach the cubs how to hunt and stay safe in the wild. Just as a mother cheetah would give her cubs wounded prey to learn how to kill, Simon dragged a dummy rabbit on a string for them to chase! Eventually the cubs had learned enough skills to survive on a wildlife reserve.

# What threats do cheetahs face?

Cheetahs face a variety of threats, all of which have led to them becoming endangered. Cheetah population numbers have dropped for a number of reasons.

## Habitat destruction

A single cheetah needs a large area of land to hunt and find the prey it needs to survive. Unfortunately, cheetahs' typical habitat is increasingly being used for building and farming. The space the cheetahs have left to hunt in is getting much smaller and they are having to compete more with other predators. This means there are fewer prey animals left for cheetahs to hunt. **Climate change** is also affecting cheetahs' habitats, as the surroundings that cheetahs need to survive are changing or disappearing and the number of prey animals is decreasing.

## How many cheetahs?

This chart shows how drastically the number of cheetahs in the wild has fallen.

| | |
|---|---|
| 1900 | **10,000** cheetahs in 33 African countries. **70–110** cheetahs in Iran. |
| 1975 | **30,000** cheetahs in Africa. Only **200** cheetahs in Iran. |
| 2000 | **12,500** cheetahs in 26 African countries. Only **100** cheetahs in Iran. |

## Vulnerable cat

Cheetahs find it hard to compete with larger predators, which will take their food and kill their cubs. As a group, they are also at risk from disease or changes in the environment because they are all so similar genetically. Other species have more genetic variation and so some animals are stronger or have more resistance to disease than others. Cheetahs, on the other hand, can all be affected by the same problems, so one disease could wipe out many.

These illegal cheetah furs have been seized by the authorities.

## HUMAN THREATS

**Poachers** hunt and kill cheetahs illegally for their fur while in some places farmers shoot cheetahs if they think they threaten their livestock. Even tourists can be a threat to cheetah numbers if safari vehicles scare the animals away from their kills before they have had time to feed. While many safari companies are careful not to disturb wild animals, some tourists can get too close and separate a mother from her cubs.

# How can people help cheetahs?

Many people and organizations are working hard to help protect cheetahs.

When population numbers for a particular species become low, the Convention of International Trade in Endangered Species (CITES) registers them to alert governments, conservationists, and the public. CITES has classified African cheetahs as vulnerable and cheetahs in Iran as critically endangered.

## The Iranian Cheetah Project

There are thought to be only 70 to 110 cheetahs left in Iran, living on a remote plateau in the centre of the country. The Iranian Department of the Environment is working with conservation organizations to prevent these cheetahs becoming extinct. It has set up five special reserves, protected by guards, and has **campaigned** to encourage Iranians to protect cheetahs.

### TAKING ACTION

Several African countries, including Namibia and Kenya, have developed special action plans to protect cheetahs. Other strategies have been developed by whole regions working together, such as in Eastern and Southern Africa. These action plans aim to improve the monitoring of cheetah numbers and exchange information about them more effectively. Governments are also considering the effect of any new land development on cheetah populations.

These rangers work to protect animals on a national park in Kenya.

## African wildlife reserves

African governments have also set up national parks and wildlife **reserves** to protect endangered animals. These include the Serengeti National Park in Tanzania, the Masai Mara National Reserve in Kenya, and the Kruger National Park in South Africa. However, although these parks and reserves provide protected spaces for wildlife, cheetah populations have not increased because within these areas they face too much competition from larger predators, such as lions and hyenas. This competition has led to many cheetahs leaving protected areas to live on farmland where they face threats from humans.

## Conservation organizations

As well as governments, many conservation groups are working to protect cheetahs. These include the World Wildlife Foundation (WWF), Panthera, the Cheetah Conservation Fund in Namibia, and the Cheetah Conservation Foundation in South Africa. These groups raise awareness of cheetahs' endangered status in countries where cheetahs live and around the world. They also work hard to raise money to help protect cheetahs. For example, members of the public can donate money to 'adopt' a cheetah. By doing this, they not only help to protect the animals and their habitat but they also receive information about cheetahs and the difficulties they face and so become more educated about these and other wild animals.

## Research

Scientists studying cheetahs in the wild and in captivity also play an important part in helping protect them. The research these scientists do helps us to understand the causes of population decline. Scientists who carry out research over a number of years are able to advise governments and conservation groups on how best to help cheetahs.

### DR LAURIE MARKER

Dr Laurie Marker is an American scientist who began working with cheetahs in 1974. In 1990, she set up the Cheetah Conservation Fund and moved to Namibia to develop a research centre. Her work has helped to educate people in Namibia about cheetahs, as well as promote captive breeding programmes around the world. She has won many awards for her work, which has helped to protect cheetah populations in Namibia and other countries.

This woman works to help cheetahs with the Cheetah Conservation Fund in Namibia.

# What does the future hold for cheetahs?

The future for cheetahs does not look good if their habitat continues to shrink. They will struggle to survive if they don't have the space they need to live, hunt, and raise cubs. In the future, climate change may present another threat if numbers of the prey animals that cheetahs need to eat are reduced. Without help and protection, the cheetah is unlikely to survive for more than a few decades.

## Namibian success story

In Namibia, the Cheetah Conservation Fund (CCF) has worked with farmers over many years. The largest population of cheetahs is found in Namibia. When cheetahs started to leave reserves and live on farmland, they came into conflict with farmers who saw them as a threat to cattle and would often shoot them. In the 1990s, the CCF began educating farmers to help avoid this, for example by using guard dogs to protect cattle instead of shooting cheetahs. By showing the human population that they can live alongside cheetahs, CCF's work has helped to stop the fall in cheetah numbers in Namibia, where 2,500 to 3,000 cheetahs currently live.

This farmer is using a guard dog to protect his goats from cheetahs and in turn is helping to protect the cheetahs themselves.

## Hope for the future

One way people are helping to increase cheetah numbers is by breeding them in captivity and then releasing them into the wild. This helps to bring a range of cheetahs that aren't too closely related together to mate and produce stronger offspring in the future. If enough people learn about cheetahs today and want to help them, we can hope that these beautiful cats will survive in the future.

Many organizations and governments are working to protect cheetahs.

# Cheetah profile

| | |
|---|---|
| **Species:** | Cheetah |
| **Latin name:** | *Acinonyx jubatus* |
| **Length:** | 1.2 metres (4 feet) |
| **Weight:** | 34–54 kilograms (75–119 pounds) |
| **Tail length:** | 65–85 centimetres (2–3 feet) |
| **Habitat:** | Grasslands, open plains, rocky uplands, and woodlands of Africa and central Iran |
| **Diet:** | Smaller antelope, such as Thompson's gazelle, impala, and springbok, as well as smaller animals, such as rabbits, birds, and warthogs |
| **Range:** | Parts of Africa and small parts of the Middle East |
| **Gestation period:** | About 100 days |
| **Number of cubs per litter:** | Around four to eight cubs. Females are around 22 months old when they are ready to have cubs and give birth about once every two years. |
| **Life expectancy:** | About 12 years |

Long spine and long legs help the cheetah run very fast.

Its slim build means the cheetah is light and agile.

Powerful eyes can see long distances.

Cheetahs have excellent hearing.

Thin fur keeps the cheetah cool when hunting.

Large nostrils allow the cheetah to breathe in lots of air when running.

A cheetah's long tail helps it to balance when running.

Sandy colour and spotted coat are useful camouflage when hunting.

Hard paw pads and claws help the cheetah to grip the ground as it runs.

# Glossary

**adaptation** body part or behaviour of a living thing that helps it survive in a particular habitat

**amputee** person who has had legs or arms removed

**binocular vision** using both eyes together to see

**camouflaged** able to blend in with the environment and hide

**campaign** take part in activities to spread a message and get support

**classify** group living things together by their similarities and differences

**climate change** rise in temperature of Earth's atmosphere

**coalition** group of young male cheetahs

**consumer** animal that eats plants or other animals

**decoy** something that lures a threat away

**dewclaw** extra claw on some animals that lies higher up the leg than other claws

**diurnal** active during the day

**evolve** change gradually over time

**faeces** poo

**food chain** sequence in which one creature eats another, which eats another, and so on

**food web** network of intertwined food chains

**genetic** to do with genes or inherited characteristics

**groom** clean an animal's fur

**habitat** type of place or surroundings that a living thing prefers to live in

**home range** area in which an animal usually lives

**instinct** natural tendency or way of behaving

**mantle** area of thick, raised hair on a cub's neck and back

**mate** come together to reproduce or have young

**migrate** move from one place to another

**muzzle** front of an animal's face, made up of the nose and mouth

**oxygen** gas in the air that is needed for animals to live

**poacher** person who hunts animals illegally

**predator** animal that hunts and kills another animal for food

**prey** animal that is hunted and killed for food by another animal

**producer** plant in a food chain that makes food

**reproduce** to have offspring

**reserve** special area where wild animals are protected

**savannah** large area of grassland with scattered trees

**scavenger** animal that feeds on dead animals

**sinus** cavity in the face

**species** group of similar living things that can mate with each other

**spine** backbone

**territory** area of land that an animal claims as its own

**urine** liquid waste from an animal

# Find out more

## Books

*Countdown to Extinction*, David Burnie (Oxford University Press, 2008)

*Face to Face with Cheetahs* (Face to Face with Animals), Chris Johns and Elizabeth Carney (National Geographic Society, 2008)

*ZSL Big Cats*, Michael Cox (Bloomsbury Childrens, 2012)

## Websites

The Cheetah Conservation Fund
**www.cheetah.org**
This website is full of information about cheetahs and the threats they face. There is a special section for kids with information about how you can help to protect cheetahs.

BBC Nature
**www.bbc.co.uk/nature/life/ cheetah**
Visit this website to watch videos of cheetahs in the wild.

## Organizations

### The World Wildlife Fund
www.wwf.org.uk
WWF works to protect animals and nature, and needs your help! Have a look at their website and see what you can do.

### The Born Free Foundation
www.bornfree.org
This charity works to protect cheetahs and many other endangered wild animals.

## Places to visit

### Chester Zoo
www.chesterzoo.org
Visit Chester Zoo to see cheetahs in captivity and find out more about these and other big cats.

### Whipsnade Zoo
www.zsl.org/zsl-whipsnade-zoo
Over the last 40 years, over 130 cheetah cubs have been born and raised at Whipsnade Zoo. If you are lucky, you will see cubs when you visit.

# Index